label cards

Marjolein Zweed

FORTE PUBLISHERS

Contents

ISBN 90 5877 379 5

This is a publication from
Forte Publishers BV
P.O. Box 1394
3500 BJ Utrecht
The Netherlands

For more information about the creative books available from Forte Publishers:
www.hobby-party.com

Publisher: Els Neele
Editor: Gina Kors-Lambers
Photography and digital image editing: Piet Pulles Fotografie, Waalwijk, the Netherlands
Cover and inner design:
BADE creatieve communicatie, Baarn, the Netherlands
Translation: TextCase, Hilversum, the Netherlands

Preface

"Label cards" is my third book, and I've designed new 3D sheets, cutting papers and this time scrapbook sheets as well. The scrapbook sheets are meant to decorate your photo albums, but they can also be used to make cards. There are labels and memo pages for writing your personal messages, as well as letters for sticking your own texts and names on the cards. To make labels, I used not only the sheets, but also charms and eyelet tags. They're so much fun to work with! There are also gift labels in this book, for putting on a gift or a bouquet of flowers.

Have fun making the cards and gift labels!

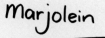

Marjolein

All the examples in this book can be seen in my shop in Abbekerk (the Netherlands), "Marjolein Zweed Creatief".

Techniques

Card stock and cutting papers

Boxes cut from cutting papers and card stock are used on the cards. Their slightly different sizes give you subtle borders. Always be careful when selecting the right colour of card stock. The right colour combination of card stock, the cutting papers and pictures make the card a harmonious whole. The card stock and the cutting papers are best cut using a ruler.

3D

The cards in this book are finished in 3D. This means that several layers of the same picture are glued right on top of each other. Using 3D glue or 3D foam tape between the layers creates depth and gives the card a three-dimensional effect. The cards in this book are worked in two, three or four layers. You'll need as many 3D-sheets as the number of layers you want to use. Each chapter has an indication of how many layers the cards have.
Most of the chapters have an illustration of the 3D cutting scheme. Of course, you can use more or fewer layers if you like. I usually cut out the straight edges of the pictures.
I usually stick the first (bottom) layer on with photo glue. You can use 3D glue or 3D foam tape for the remaining layers. Try out a few ways until you find the one that you like best. This often is very personal. Before you glue on the pictures, you may want to bring them into shape a bit with your fingers.

If you use 3D glue, it's best to use a syringe so that it's easier to measure a dose. Put a few drops of 3D glue on the back of the picture. Carefully place it on top of the previous picture. Don't press down too hard or it will lose its depth. Continue with the following layers. Let it dry thoroughly before you send the card. 3D foam tape is available in blocks or in a roll so you can cut small pieces yourself. These small pieces of tape can be stuck on the back of the picture. Put this on top of the previous one. Position it right the first time, because you won't be able to move it after you've stuck it down! Continue with the remaining layers.

Eyelets

Craft eyelets are just like the round ones on your shoes, but all kinds of figures are available besides the round eyelets, such as hearts and flowers (see photo 1).
Eyelets are fastened on using an eyelet tool consisting of three parts; a shaft and two

1. Various eyelets, eyelet tool set and eyelet mat.

2. Punch holes using the eyelet tool.

3. Punch eyelets closed on the back side.

4. The eyelets are set.

attachments which can be screwed on. One is used to punch a hole, and the other (with the bump) fixes the eyelets.

If you're punching a hole in your card, make sure that it's open, otherwise you'll punch a hole in the back side as well. Lay the card on an eyelet mat or old cutting mat. Never use your good cutting mat, because using an eyelet tool will pit it. Set the eyelet tool, with the hole punching attachment, on the card. Using a hammer, hit the back end of the shaft (see photo 2). Put an eyelet through the hole that you've just made. Set the eyelet tool with the other attachment on the back side of the eyelet. Hit the shaft again with the hammer (see photo 3). The eyelet is now fastened (see photo 4). If you're going to make a hole in the upper left corner of a gift label, make a hole in the back at the same time. Put an eyelet through the hole on the front side and set.

Eyelets can also be used to set in eyelet tags. These are little metal figures. Before putting the eyelet through the hole, place an eyelet tag on the hole. Now put the eyelet through both holes and hammer it closed.

Charms

Charms are small metal decorations. They are attached with mini split pins or paper fasteners (bradletz). Place the charm where you want it and mark the holes. Remove the charm and make small holes with the points of your scissors. Replace the charm and insert the cotter pins through the holes. Bend the two ends apart at the back side.

Materials

- 3D scissors
- cutting knife
- cutting mat
- transparent cutting ruler (Securit)
- photo glue
- 3D glue with syringe
- 3D foam tape
- Marjolein's 3D-sheets
  Each sheet contains several blocks in different sizes.
- Marjolein's cutting papers
  This series of papers goes well with the Marjolein's 3D sheets. Each sheet has 2 designs co-ordinated with each other.
- Marjolein's scrapbook sheets
  These sheets can be used to decorate your photo album or scrapbook. But, as you can see from this book, they're also wonderful for making cards.
- Papicolor or other card stock (colour numbers given are Papicolor numbers)
  You can cut your own cards from this card stock, but the regular and square cards are available pre-cut and folded. The colour numbers indicated at the beginning of each chapter are Papicolor numbers.
- tools for setting eyelets:
  eyelet tool set (mini), eyelet mat and hammer

Any other materials needed are indicated in their respective chapters.

Card on page 3

What you'll need: see Ducks

Take a 13 cm square double lavender card and glue a 13 cm square of cutting paper no. 7, a 10.5 cm square of nut-brown card stock and a 10 cm square of cutting paper no. 7. Cut out a large brown label, glue onto nut brown card stock and cut out again, leaving a narrow border around the label. Glue a duck sticker (smallest size) on the label. Cut 25 cm of cord (2 mm), string it through the label and make a knot in it. Glue the label onto the card with 3D foam tape or 3D glue. Glue two large patchwork pieces onto the card. Work the duck in 3D. Using 3D glue or 3D foam tape, glue on two buttons and the folded-over corner of the label onto the card.

Pansies

Pansies are always good

on birthday cards.

What you'll need:
- ❏ *3D sheet of purple pansies (4 layers)*
- ❏ *cutting papers: no. 9 and no. 12*
- ❏ *scrapbook sheets:*
  brown memo pad and brown alphabet
- ❏ *Papicolor card stock:*
  lilac (37) and carnation white (03)
- ❏ *text charms*
- ❏ *bradletz, mini silver*
- ❏ *mini eyelets, ivory*
- ❏ *brown identipen*
- ❏ *cream ribbon*

Card 1

Take a regular double lilac card (10.5 x 15 cm).
Fold a 15 x 21 cm piece of cutting paper no. 9
double and glue it around the card. Glue a 12 x
7.5 cm piece of cutting paper no. 12 and an 11.5 x
7 cm piece of cutting paper no. 9 on the card.
Glue a medium-size pansy on the card and your
message using the letters. Work the pansy in 3D.

Card 2

Take a regular double carnation white card
(10.5 x 15 cm). Fold a 15 x 21 cm piece of cutting
paper no. 12 double and glue it around the card.
Glue a 6.5 cm square of cutting paper no. 9 and
a 6 cm square of cutting paper no. 12 on the
card. Glue a pansy (largest size) in the lower left
corner, and a pansy (smallest size) in the upper
right corner. Fasten a charm onto the card. Work
the pansies in 3D.

Card 3

Cut two 14 x 5 cm strips, one from carnation
white card stock and one from cutting paper
no. 12. Glue the strips together and fold them
double, with the cutting paper facing out.
Glue on a pansy (middle size), and the numbers
you wish. Fasten a regular eyelet in the upper
left corner. Cut off 30 cm of ribbon, string it
through the card and tie it in a bow. Work the
pansy in 3D.

Card 4

Cut out two 14 x 5 cm strips of lilac card stock
and cutting paper no. 9. Glue the strips together
and fold them double, with the cutting paper
facing out. Glue on a pansy (smallest size) and
a small label. Place a text sticker on the label.
Set a regular eyelet in the upper left corner.
Cut 30 cm of ribbon, string it through the card

2.

3.

4.

5.

6.

Card 6

Take a regular double lilac card (10.5 x 15 cm). Fold a 15 x 21 cm piece of cutting paper no. 9 double and stick it around the card. Glue a 12 x 7.5 cm piece of cutting paper no. 12, and an 11.5 x 7 cm piece of cutting paper no. 9 on the card. Cut out a rectangular memo sheet (largest size) and stick on a pansy (smallest size). Write your text on the memo sheet with an identipen. Glue the memo and a pansy (largest size) on the card. Work the pansies in 3D.

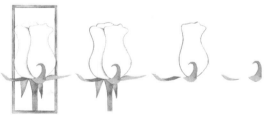

and make a bow. Fasten a regular eyelet in the eye of the label. Work the pansy in 3D.

Card 5

Take a 13 cm square double lilac card and stick a 13 cm square of cutting paper no. 9 onto it. Cut a 10.5 cm square of cutting paper no. 12 and a 10 cm square of cutting paper no. 9 and stick together. Glue four pansies (middle size) on the frame. Set a charm on the frame. Glue the frame onto the card. Work the pansies in 3D.

White roses and anemones

These 3D designs can also be combined with the "anniversary" set to make lovely wedding cards.

What you'll need:
- ❏ *3D sheets: white roses and anemones (2 to 4 layers)*
- ❏ *cutting papers: design nos. 11 and 12*
- ❏ *scrapbook sheets: green anniversary numbers and brown memo sheets*
- ❏ *Papicolor card stock: olive green (45), carnation white (03), caramel (26) and light green (47)*
- ❏ *eyelets: fun green*
- ❏ *eyelet tags: open fun figures*
- ❏ *charms: wedding and text*
- ❏ *bradletz: mini cotter pins (silver)*
- ❏ *golden text sticker or alphabet*
- ❏ *cream ribbon*

Card 1
Cut a 21 cm square from carnation white card stock and fold in half. Glue on a 10.5 x 21 cm piece of cutting paper no. 12. Cut a 6.5 x 16.5 cm strip of card stock and a 6 x 16 cm piece of cutting paper no. 12 and glue together. Glue two anemone pictures (second smallest size) and an anniversary number (largest size). Fasten a text charm onto the frame. Glue the frame onto the card. Work the anemones in 3D.

Card 2
Take a regular double carnation white card (10.5 x 15 cm). Fold a 15 x 21 cm piece of cutting paper no. 11 in half and glue it over the card. Cut a 7 x 10.5 cm piece of olive green card stock and a 6.5 x 10 cm piece of caramel card stock and glue together. Cut out three pieces from cutting paper no. 11, 1.5 x 3 cm, 3 x 3 cm and 4.5 x 3 cm. Glue the three pieces of cutting paper, an anemone picture (smallest size), a picture of rings (smallest size) and a number (smallest size) in this frame. Fix the charms on the frame. Glue the frame onto the card. Work the anemone in 3D (2 layers).

Card 3
Take a 13 cm square carnation-white double card and glue a 13 cm square of cutting paper no. 11 on top. Glue a picture of an anemone (largest size) onto it. Set plain eyelets in the corners. Work the anemone in 3D. If using glue,

let it dry well before putting on the label. Cut out a small brown label and stick on a text sticker. Fasten a plain eyelet in the eye of the label. Cut off 30 cm of ribbon, thread it through the hole in the label and tie it to the stem of the anemone. Fasten down the label with 3D glue or 3Dfoam tape.

Card 4

Cut two 13 x 5 cm strips, one from carnation white card stock and one from cutting paper no. 11. Glue the strips together. Fold over at 5 cm, with the green side facing outwards. This will be easiest if you score the fold line first. Glue on an anemone (next to smallest size). Cut two rings (smallest size) from the sheet of numbers and glue them on the long bit of the card sticking out. Set a plain eyelet in the upper left corner of the card. Cut off a 30 cm length of ribbon, thread it through the card and tie it in a bow. Work the anemone in 3D.

Card 5

Cut two 14 x 5 cm strips, one from carnation white card stock and one from cutting paper no. 12. Glue the two together. Fold over, with the cutting paper facing outwards. Glue an anemone (smallest size) on the left side, and an anniver-sary number on the right. Glue a text sticker on the lower edge. Affix a plain eyelet in the upper left corner of the card. Cut off a 30 cm length of ribbon, thread it through the card and tie it in a bow. Work the anemone in 3D (2 layers).

Card 6

Take a 13 cm square carnation white double card and stick a 13 cm square of cutting paper no. 12 on it. Cut a 10.5 cm square of olive green card stock and a 10 cm square piece of cutting paper no. 12 and stick them together. Set an eyelet tag in one corner of the frame using a plain eyelet. Glue the frame onto the card. Glue an anemone (second smallest size), a picture of rings (largest size) and an anniversary number (largest size) on the card. Work the anemone in 3D.

Card 7

Take a plain carnation white double card (10.5 x 15 cm). Fold a 15 x 21 cm piece of cutting paper no. 12 in half and stick around the card. Glue the large picture of a rose onto this. Glue a picture of the rings (largest size) on the card. Fasten two eyelets onto a heart. Work the rose in 3D.

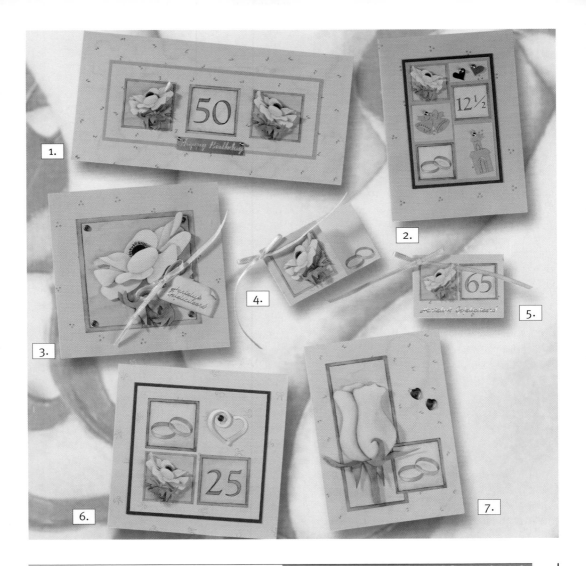

Daisies

These cards are perfect for your friends with green thumbs.

What you'll need:
- ❏ *3D sheet: daisies (2 layers)*
- ❏ *cutting papers: design nos. 10 and 11*
- ❏ *scrapbook sheet: blue memo pages*
- ❏ *Papicolor card stock: lavender (21), olive green (45), light green (47) and dark blue (41)*
- ❏ *charms: garden and text*
- ❏ *bradletz: mini silver*
- ❏ *eyelets: fun light blue*
- ❏ *eyelet tags: open fun figures*
- ❏ *blue identipen*
- ❏ *silver text sticker or alphabet*
- ❏ *waxed plain cotton cord: 1 and 2 mm*
- ❏ *raffia*

Card 1

Take a 13 cm square double light green card and stick a 13 cm square of cutting paper no. 11 onto it. Cut a 10.5 cm square of cutting paper no. 10 and a 10 cm square of cutting paper no. 11 and stick them together. In the upper right corner of the frame, set an eyelet tag (in the shape of a flower) using an eyelet (in the shape of a tiny flower). Glue the frame onto the card. Glue three daisies (middle size) onto the card. Work the daisies in 3D.

Card 2

Cut two 12 x 5 cm-strips from lavender card stock and cutting paper no. 10. Glue the two strips together. Fold over at 5 cm, with the cutting paper facing outwards. This will be easier if you score the fold line first. Put a daisy picture (middle size) on the short side. Cut out a butterfly and stick onto the piece of the card that protrudes. Affix a plain eyelet in the upper left corner of the card. Cut off 20 cm of cord (1 mm), thread it through the card and knot it. Work the daisy in 3D.

Card 3

Take a plain double lavender card (10.5 x 15 cm). Fold a 15 x 21 cm piece of cutting paper no. 10 over and stick around the card. Cut a 4.5 x 15 cm strip of olive green card stock and a 4 x 15 cm strip of cutting paper no. 11 and stick the two together. Cut three daisies (smallest size) and glue onto the strip. Put a watering can charm on the strip. Glue the strip on the card 1 cm from the lower edge. Glue on two butterflies and work the daisies in 3D.

Card 4

Take a plain double light green card (10.5 x 15 cm). Fold a 15 x 21 cm piece of cutting paper no. 11 in half and glue around the card. Glue the long strip with daisies (largest size) onto it. Put on a sticker and a butterfly. Fasten a birdhouse charm onto the card. Work the butterflies and the daisies in 3D.

Card 5

Cut two 14 x 5 cm strips from light green card stock and from cutting paper no. 11. Glue the strips together and fold double, with the cutting paper facing outwards. Glue on a daisy (smallest size) and a small label. Put a text sticker on the label. Set a plain eyelet in the upper left corner of the card. Cut off 20 cm of cord (1 mm), thread it through the card and tie a knot in it. Fasten a regular eyelet in the hole of the label. Work the daisy in 3D.

Card 6

Take a 13 cm square double lavender card and stick on a 13 cm square of cutting paper no. 10. Cut a 9 cm square of dark blue card stock and an 8.5 cm square of cutting paper no. 10 and glue together. Glue a daisy (largest size) on the frame. Set a text charm on the frame. Glue the frame onto the card. Cut out a large blue label, glue it onto dark blue card stock and cut it out again, leaving a narrow border around it. Cut out and glue a daisy picture (smallest size) onto the label. Cut off 25 cm cord (2 mm), thread it onto the label and make a knot in it. Fasten the label to the card with 3D foam tape or 3D glue. Work the daisies in 3D. Fasten another folded-over corner of the label to the card using 3D glue or 3D foam tape.

1.

2.

3.

4.

5.

6.

7.

Ducks

Personalise your cards by putting the child's name on them.

What you'll need:
- ❏ scrapbook sheets:
  pink ducks (2 layers), blue ducks (2 layers),
  patchwork alphabet and
  brown memo pages
- ❏ cutting paper nos. 7, 8 and 12
- ❏ Card stock: light pink (23), cherry (33),
  nut brown (39), lavender (21) and
  dark blue (41)
- ❏ charms: baby and text
- ❏ bradletz: mini silver
- ❏ eyelets: mini ivory
- ❏ brown identipen
- ❏ cream ribbon
- ❏ plain cotton cord: 1 and 2 mm

3D: To give the ducks a 3D effect, glue on a second layer of head and wings.

Card 1
Cut a 21 cm square from light pink card stock and fold double. Glue on a 21 x 10.5 cm piece of cutting paper no. 8, a 6.5 x 16.5 cm piece of cerise card stock and a 6 x 16 cm piece of cutting paper no. 8. Glue the letters of the name onto the card with photo glue. Using 3D glue or 3D foam tape, glue the duck (middle size) onto the card and work the 3D.

Card 2
Take a regular double lavender card (10.5 x 15 cm). Fold a 15 x 21 cm piece of cutting paper no. 7 double and glue around the card. Cut a 6.5 cm square from dark blue card stock. Glue on three letters, one large and two small patchwork pieces. Fasten a stroller charm onto the frame. Glue the frame onto the card. Using 3D glue or 3D foam tape glue a button onto a small patchwork piece.

Card 3
Take a regular double carnation white card (10.5 x 15 cm). Fold a 15 x 21 cm piece of cutting paper no. 12 double and glue it around the card. Using photo glue, glue a duck (middle size), two small ducks, two small patchwork pieces and four letters onto the card. Using brown identipen draw a line for the ducks to sit on. Glue on six buttons using 3D glue or 3D foam tape. Work the ducks in 3D.

Card 4

Take a regular double light pink card (10.5 x 15 cm). Fold a 15 x 21 cm piece of cutting paper no. 8 double and glue it around the card. Cut a 12.5 x 8.5 cm piece of cherry card stock and a 12 x 8 cm piece of cutting paper no. 12 and stick them together. Glue letters and large and small patchwork pieces on this frame. Fasten a text charm and baby charms onto the frame. Glue the frame onto the card. Using photo glue, glue a safety pin and, using 3D glue or 3D foam tape, buttons onto the card.

Card 5

Take a 13 cm square light pink double card and glue a 13 cm square of cutting paper no. 8. Cut a 10.5 cm square of cherry card stock and a 10 cm square of cutting paper no. 8 and stick them together. Glue a duck (largest size) onto the card. Fasten a text charm onto the frame. Glue the frame onto the card. Using 3D glue or 3D foam tape glue two buttons onto the duck. Work the duck in 3D.

Card 6

Cut two 13 x 5 cm strips, from light pink card stock and from cutting paper no. 8. Glue the two strips together. Fold over at 5 cm, with the cutting paper facing outwards. This will be easier if you score the fold line first. Glue a large patchwork piece on the short side. Glue two patchwork pieces on the piece of card sticking out. Set a regular eyelet in the upper left corner. Cut off a 30 cm length of ribbon, thread it through the card and tie it in a bow. Using 3D glue or 3D foam tape glue a duck onto the large patchwork piece and work it in 3D. Glue a safety pin onto one small patchwork piece using photo glue, and use 3D glue or 3D foam tape to put a button onto the other piece.

Card 7

Cut two 14 x 5 cm strips, from carnation white card stock and from cutting paper no. 12. Glue the two strips together and fold in half, with the cutting paper facing outwards. Glue on one large and two small patchwork pieces. Fasten a regular eyelet in the upper left corner. Cut off a 30 cm length of ribbon, thread it through the card and tie it in a bow. Using 3D glue or 3D foam tape, glue a button on the large heart.

Pink tulips

Tulips are my favourite flowers. This time I've painted them pink.

What you'll need:
- ❏ *3D-sheet of pink tulips (3 layers)*
- ❏ *cutting papers: designs 8 and 11*
- ❏ *scrapbook sheets: green anniversary numbers and brown memo pages*
- ❏ *Card stock: light green (47), lilac (14) and olive green (45)*
- ❏ *mosaic punch*
- ❏ *paste-on gemstones: pink*
- ❏ *eyelets: fun pink*
- ❏ *eyelet tags: open fun figures*
- ❏ *text charms*
- ❏ *mini silver bradletz*
- ❏ *gold text stickers*
- ❏ *cream ribbon*

Card 1

Take a regular double lilac card (10.5 x 15 cm). Cut a 6.5 x 11 cm piece of olive green card stock and a 6 x 10.5 cm piece of cutting paper no. 11 and glue them together. Fasten two heart eyelets in the lower-left corner of this piece, and glue it onto the card. Cut out one large and one small brown label. Glue the labels onto lilac card stock and cut out again, with a small border around them. On the smallest label glue a text sticker and on the largest a pink tulip (smallest size). Glue the labels together at an angle. Set a regular eyelet in the eye of each label. Cut off a 30 cm length of ribbon, thread through the labels and tie it in a bow. Using 3D foam tape or 3D glue, glue the labels onto the card. Work the tulip in 3D.

Card 2

Cut a 21 cm square from light green card stock and fold in half. Glue on a 6.5 x 16.5 cm strip of lilac card stock and a 6 x 16 cm strip from cutting paper no. 11. Glue on three pink tulips (second smallest size). In the lower right corner put on an eyelet tag (in the shape of a flower), using an eyelet (flower). Fasten a regular eyelet in the each of the other corners. Work the tulips in 3D.

Card 3

Cut a 14 x 5 cm strip from lilac card stock and fold in half. Glue a pink tulip (smallest size) on the left side, and an anniversary number on the right. Put a text sticker on the lower edge.

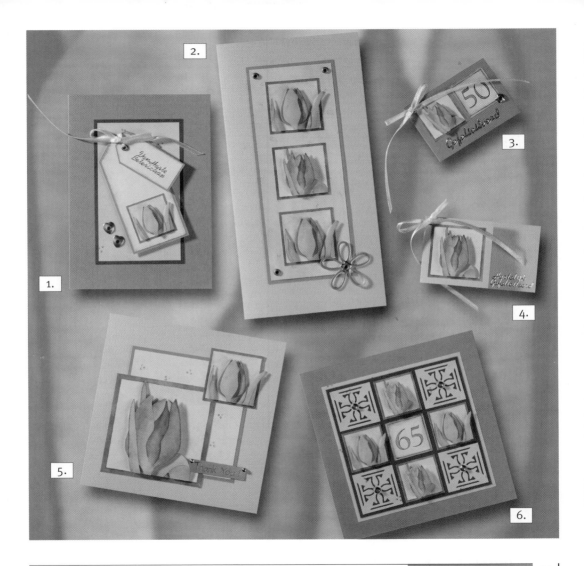

Fasten a regular eyelet in the upper left corner. Cut off a 30 cm length of ribbon, thread it through the card and tie it in a bow. Set a flower-shaped eyelet in the lower right corner of the number. Work the tulip in 3D.

Card 4

Cut a 13.5 x 5 cm strip from light green card stock and fold over at 5 cm. This is easier if you score the line slightly before folding. On the short side put a pink tulip (second smallest size) and a text sticker on the long side. (If your text sticker is longer, you'll have to start with a

longer strip.) Set a regular eyelet in the upper left corner. Cut off a 30 cm length of ribbon, thread it through the card and tie it in a bow. Work the tulip in 3D.

Card 5

Take a 13 cm square double light green card and glue on a 9 cm square of lilac card stock and an 8.5 cm square of cutting paper no. 8. Glue a pink tulip (largest size) in the lower left corner and in the upper right a pink tulip (second smallest size). Fasten a charm on the card. Work the tulips in 3D.

Card 6

Take a 13 cm square double lilac card and glue on a 10.5 cm square piece of cutting paper no. 11 and a 10 cm square of olive green card stock. Punch four mosaic sections from cutting paper no. 11 and cut into 3 cm squares. Glue the mosaic squares, four pink tulips (smallest size) and an anniversary number (smallest size) onto the card. Decorate the mosaic squares with paste-on gems. Work the tulips in 3D.

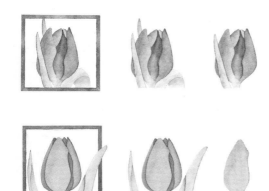

Strawberries

These cards are good for
birthdays, but also do well
as get-well cards.

What you'll need:
- ❏ *3D sheet: strawberries (2 or 3 layers)*
- ❏ *cutting paper design no. 11*
- ❏ *scrapbook sheets: green anniversary*
  numbers and brown memo pages
- ❏ *card stock: fiesta red (12), light green (47)*
  and olive green (45)
- ❏ *eyelets: fun green*
- ❏ *eyelet tags: labels & frames*
- ❏ *silver text sticker or alphabet*
- ❏ *brown identipen*
- ❏ *waxed plain cotton cord: 1 and 2 mm*

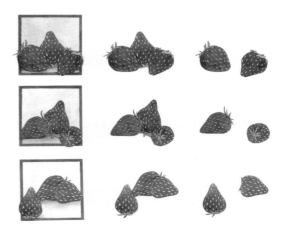

Card 1

Take a regular double light green card (10.5 x
15 cm). Fold a 15 x 21 cm piece of cutting paper
no. 11 double and glue around the card. Glue a
4.5 x 15 cm strip of fiesta red card stock at 1 cm
from the right edge of the card. Glue onto that a
4 x 15 cm strip of cutting paper no. 11. On the
strip glue three pictures of strawberries (smallest size) and an anniversary number (smallest
size) and work the strawberries in 3D. Using 3D
glue or 3D foam tape glue a strawberry in the
lower left corner of the card.

Card 2

Take a 13 cm square double light green card
and glue a 13 cm square piece of cutting paper
no. 11 onto it. Cut a 10.5 cm square of olive
green card stock and a 10 cm square of cutting
paper no. 11 and glue them together. Set two
flower eyelets in the upper right area of the
frame. Glue this frame onto the card. Cut out
a square memo page (smallest size) and glue
onto olive green card stock. Cut out again, with
a narrow border around it. Glue a picture of
strawberries (smallest size) on the memo page.
Write your text on the memo page with the
identipen and glue the page on the card. Work

the strawberries in 3D. Cut out more straw-berries, glue onto the card and work in 3D.

Card 3

Cut two 14 x 5 cm strips, from light green card stock and from cutting paper no. 11. Glue the two strips together and fold in half, with the cutting paper facing outwards. Glue on a picture of strawberries (middle size). Cut out a few separate strawberries and glue them on. Set a square eyelet in the upper left corner. Cut 20 cm of cord (1 mm), thread it through the card and knot it. Work the strawberries in 3D.

Card 4

Take a 13 cm square double fiesta red card and glue on a 10.5 cm square of olive green card stock and a 10 cm square of cutting paper no. 11. Glue a picture of strawberries (largest size) onto the card. Cut out a large brown label, glue onto fiesta red card stock and cut out again, leaving a narrow border. Glue a picture of strawberries (middle size) onto the label. Cut off 25 cm cord (2 mm), thread it onto the label and knot it. Using 3D foam tape or 3D glue, glue the labels onto the card. Work the strawberries in 3D.

Card 5

Take a regular double light green card (10.5 x 15 cm). Fold a 15 x 21 cm piece of cutting paper no. 11 in half and glue around the card. Cut a 12 x 7.5 cm piece of fiesta red card stock and an 11.5 x 7 cm piece of cutting paper no. 11 and glue together. Set an eyelet tag in the lower right corner of the box and mark the position of the eyelets. Fasten the eyelet tag with regular eyelets. Glue a text sticker in the frame. Glue the frame onto the card. Glue on a picture of strawberries (largest size) and work them in 3D.

Card 6

Cut a 14 x 5 cm strip from fiesta red card stock and fold in half. Glue on a 6.5 x 4.5 cm piece of cutting paper no. 11. Set a regular eyelet in the upper left corner of the card. Cut 20 cm of cord (1 mm), thread it through the card and tie a knot. Glue on an anniversary number (largest size). Using 3D glue or 3D foam tape, glue a few strawberries (smallest size) on the card and work them in 3D.

1.

2.

3.

4.

5.

6.

Teatime

An invitation on one of

these cards really makes

you feel welcome.

What you'll need:
- ❑ *3D sheet: teapot and cup (3 layers)*
- ❑ *cutting papers: design nos. 4 and 12*
- ❑ *scrapbook sheets: brown alphabet and brown memo pages*
- ❑ *card stock: nut brown (39) and carnation white (03)*
- ❑ *eyelets mini ivory*
- ❑ *text charms*
- ❑ *mini silver bradletz*
- ❑ *brown identipen*
- ❑ *waxed plain cotton cord: 1 and 2 mm*

Card 1

Take a 13 cm square double carnation white card and glue on a 13 cm square of cutting paper no. 12, a 9 cm square of nut brown card stock and an 8.5 cm square of cutting paper no. 12. Glue a teapot (largest size) in the lower left corner, and a cup (second smallest size) in the upper right. Set a charm on the card. Work the teapot and cup in 3D.

Card 2

Take a 13 cm square double nut brown card and glue on a 10 cm square of cutting paper no. 4 and a 9.5 cm square of cutting paper no. 12. Cut out a large brown label, glue onto nut brown card stock and cut out again, leaving a narrow border around it. Paste a teapot picture (smallest size) on the label. Cut off 25 cm cord (2 mm), thread onto the label and tie a knot in it. Glue the label onto the card using 3D foam tape or 3D glue. Glue a teapot (second smallest size) and a cup (second smallest size) on the card and work the teapots and cup in 3D. Using 3D glue or 3D foam tape glue another folded-over corner of the label.

Card 3

Cut a 15 x 5 cm strip of nut brown card stock and fold in half. Glue a 6.5 x 4 cm piece of cutting paper no. 4 and a 6 x 3.5 cm piece of cutting paper no. 12 on it. Set a regular eyelet in the upper left corner. Cut 20 cm of cord (1 mm), thread it through the card and tie a knot in it. Using 3D glue or 3D foam tape, glue a teapot (second smallest size) and a cup (smallest size) onto the card and work in 3D.

Card 4

Cut two 13.5 x 5 cm strips, from carnation white

card stock and from cutting paper no. 12. Glue the two strips together. Fold over at 5 cm, with the cutting paper facing outwards. This will be easier if you score the fold line first. On the short side glue a picture of a teapot (second smallest size). Cut out a cup (smallest size) and paste on the piece of card sticking out underneath. Set a

regular eyelet in the upper left corner. Cut 20 cm of cord (1 mm), thread it through the card and tie a knot in it. Work the teapot and cup in 3D.

Card 5
Take a 13 cm square double carnation white card and glue on a 13 cm square of cutting

paper no. 12, a 10 cm square of cutting paper no. 4 and a 9.5 cm square of cutting paper no. 12. Glue a 2.4 x 8.5 cm strip of nut brown card stock on the card and glue the letters T, E and A onto it. Glue a teapot (second largest size) on the card and work in 3D. Using 3D glue or 3D foam tape glue a cup (second smallest size) on the card and work it in 3D.

Card 6
Take a regular double carnation white card (10.5 x 15 cm). Fold a 15 x 21 cm piece of cutting paper no. 12 in half and glue around the white card. Cut out a long memo page (smallest size) and glue onto nut brown card stock. Cut out again, leaving a narrow border. Glue a picture of a cup (smallest size) onto the memo page. Using the identipen, write your text on the memo page. Glue the memo page onto the card. Work the cup in 3D. Using 3D glue or 3D foam tape, glue a teapot (second largest size) and a cup (second smallest size) on the card and work them in 3D.

1.

2.

3.

4.

5.

6.

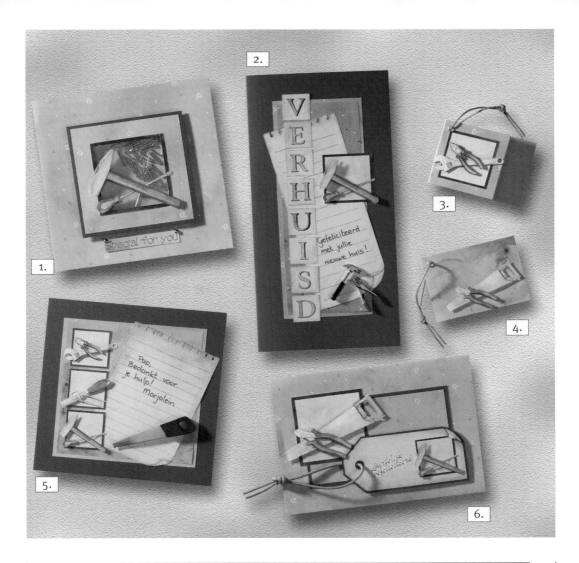

Tool set

These can be sent as "just moved" cards or birthday cards for a do-it-your-selfer.

What you'll need:
- ❏ *3D cutting sheet of tools (2 or 3 layers)*
- ❏ *cutting papers: nos. 3 and 4*
- ❏ *scrapbook sheets: brown memo pages, blue memo pages and brown alphabet*
- ❏ *card stock: brick red (35) and lavender (21)*
- ❏ *text charms*
- ❏ *mini silver bradletz*
- ❏ *eyelets: fun silver*
- ❏ *embellishment tools*
- ❏ *mica sheet*
- ❏ *small nails*
- ❏ *brown identipen*
- ❏ *silver text sticker*
- ❏ *waxed natural cotton cord 1 and 2 mm*

Card 1
Take a 13 cm square double lavender card and glue on a 13 cm square of cutting paper no. 4. Cut an 8.5 cm square of brick red card stock and an 8 cm square of cutting paper no. 4 and glue together. Glue the picture of a hammer (largest size) on top. Cut the background of the picture away. Cut a 7 cm square of mica and glue to the back of the frame by putting 3D foam tape at the edges. Make sure there are no gaps between the pieces of tape 3D foam tape. Lay a few nails on the card and glue the frame on top. Set a charm on the card. Work the tools in 3D.

Card 2
Cut a 21 cm square of brick red card stock and fold in half. Glue on a 6.5 x 16.5 cm piece of cutting paper no. 4 and a 6 x 16 cm piece of cutting paper no. 3. Cut out a long brown memo page (largest size) and write your text on it with the identipen. Glue the memo page, the letters N, E, W, H, O, M and E and a tool set picture (middle size) onto the card. Work the tools in 3D. Finish by sticking on a hammer and a pair of pliers (embellishment).

Card 3
Cut two 12 x 5 cm strips, from lavender card stock and from cutting paper no. 4. Glue the two strips together. Fold over at 5 cm, with the cutting paper facing outwards. This will be easier if you score the fold line first. Glue a picture of tools (middle size) on the short side.

Set a regular eyelet in the upper left corner. Cut 20 cm of cord (1 mm), thread it through the card and tie a knot in it. Work the tools in 3D.

Card 4

Cut two 14 x 5 cm strips, from brick red card stock and from cutting paper no. 3. Glue the two strips together and fold in half, with the cutting paper facing outwards. Set a regular eyelet in the upper left corner. Cut 20 cm of cord (1 mm), thread it through the card and tie a knot in it. Cut out the picture of a saw (middle size) and glue onto the card. Work it in 3D.

Card 5

Take a 13 cm square double brick red card and glue on a 10.5 cm square of cutting paper no. 4 and a 10 cm square of cutting paper no. 3. Cut out a blue memo page (in upper left on the sheet) and write a text on the memo page with identipen. Glue the memo page and three pictures of tools (smallest size) onto the card. Work the tools in 3D (2 layers). Finish by gluing on a saw (embellishment).

Card 6

Take a regular double lavender card (10.5 x 15 cm). Fold a 15 x 21 cm piece of cutting paper

no. 4 and glue around the card. Glue an 11 x 6.5 cm piece of brick red card stock and a 10.5 x 6 cm piece of cutting paper no. 4 on the card. Glue a picture of tools (largest size) onto the card. Cut out a large blue label, glue onto brick red card stock and cut out again, leaving a small border around it. Glue a picture of tools (smallest size) and a text sticker on the label. Cut 25 cm of cord (2 mm), thread through the label and tie a knot in it. Glue the label onto the card with 3D foam tape or 3D glue. Work the tools in 3D, using 3 layers for the largest picture and 2 for the smallest. Glue the folded-over corner of the label again with 3D glue or 3D foam tape.

Cards from cover + page 1

Card at top of cover
What you'll need: see Daisies

Take a 13 cm square double lavender card and glue on a 13 cm square of cutting paper no. 10. Cut out a blue memo page (in the upper left corner of the sheet) and write a text on the memo page with identipen. Glue the memo page and three pictures of daisies (smallest size) on the card. Glue two butterflies on the memo page with photo glue, and put a watering can (smallest size) on the card with 3D glue or 3D foam tape. Work the butterflies and daisies in 3D.

Card at bottom of cover
What you'll need: see Daisies

Take a regular double lavender card (10.5 x 15 cm). Fold a 15 x 21 cm piece of cutting paper no. 10 double and glue around the card. Cut a

12.5 x 8 cm piece of olive green card stock and a 12 x 7.5 cm piece of cutting paper no. 10 and glue together. Glue a daisy (largest size) on the box. Cut out a small blue label and put on a text sticker. Thread a piece of raffia onto the card and tie it in a bow. Using 3D glue or 3D foam tape, glue the label onto the box. Fasten rake and trowel charms onto the box. Glue onto the card and work the daisy in 3D.

Card page 1
What you'll need: see Ducks

Cut a 21 cm square from carnation white card stock and fold in half. Glue on a 21 x 10.5 cm piece of cutting paper no. 12, a 6.5 x 16.5 cm piece of nut brown card stock and a 6 x 16 cm piece of cutting paper no. 12. Glue the ducks (middle size) and the letters T, W, I, N and S onto the card with photo glue. Work the ducks in 3D.

The materials used in this book can be ordered wholesale (all addresses in the Netherlands) from: Kars & Co B.V. in Ochten • Jalekro B.V. in Assendelft • Papicolor International B.V. in Utrecht, Vadeko Kreatief in Spijkenisse • Hobby Totaal in Zwolle • Doodey-Double M Decorations in Vlijmen